SMOLDERING EMBERS OF PARADISE

T.K. Banner

AuthorHouse™
1663 Liberty Drive
Bloomington, IN 47403
www.authorhouse.com
Phone: 1 (800) 839-8640

Because of the dynamic nature of the Internet, any web addresses or links contained in this book may have changed
since publication and may no longer be valid. The views expressed in this work are solely those of the author and do
not necessarily reflect the views of the publisher, and the publisher hereby disclaims any responsibility for them.

Any people depicted in stock imagery provided by Getty Images are models,
and such images are being used for illustrative purposes only.
Certain stock imagery © Getty Images.

This book is printed on acid-free paper.

ISBN: 978-1-7283-3511-7 (sc)
ISBN: 978-1-7283-3512-4 (e)

Library of Congress Control Number: 2019918057

Print information available on the last page.

Published by AuthorHouse 11/07/2019

authorHOUSE®

SMOLDERING EMBERS

"Ruin is a gift: Ruin is the road to transformation."

Elizabeth Gilbert

ACKNOWLEGMENTS

This book could not have been written
if I did not have the support of:

My mother and fiancé who have
been my staunch supporters

Wes and Ken, my neighbors in Paradise
who became my support system

Bonnie and Ken, my friends from Paradise, who now
live nearby and help me through the recovery process

Jim's family, especially his ex-wife, who were
there for Jim and I throughout the entire ordeal

It has been two months since I completed my first book "Phoenix Rising From the Ashes." My readers have surprised me by demanding that they want "more": more insights, more information about my life. As I re-read my book, I realized that it is by no means finished; it is a reflection of life, constantly evolving and changing. I was chagrined by the fact the book still had typos when it went to the press! But it was another lesson for me: Let it go!

This past week I have been following the fires raging through California, watching homes going up in flames. My heart goes out to those who, like me, have lost everything. My son-in-law is down in Sonoma helping the firefighters and I pray for his safety. As I watch the news, I am reminded that I am not alone; there are thousands who wake up in the morning, expecting a normal routine day, only to have everything ripped from them in the ensuing hours.

My readers wanted to know what I was experiencing as I evacuated the students from the classroom the day of the fire. This memory is astonishing for me because I am a very emotional person; I fall apart at the smallest crisis. But, when we were leaving the classroom and the ashes were falling, all I could think about was the smell of the smoke in the air and trying to calm the students. I wasn't afraid: maybe because I had never had to experience any natural disasters, I didn't think about the dangerous situation we were in. Of course, the staff at the elementary school coordinated the evacuation procedure efficiently and smoothly. One by one, the students were picked up by their parents and guardians until there were just a handful of students left in the cafeteria. I still had four students from my class and we were automatically shepherded onto a school bus to take us to a nearby school. I did not even think about my car which was still in the parking lot. Somewhere in the back of my mind, the evacuation process was just another efficient fire drill! I would pick up my car at the end of the day. The reality was I had to wait over a month to see if my car was safe. The angels were with me the day I turned the corner into the parking lot of the deserted school and found my car without any residue from the smoke or fire!

I have had ample time to reflect on my situation since the fire, and the writing of my first book. I have talked to some of the survivors of the fire and some of them are literally stuck in time. Conversations seem to always center around the day of the fire, not unlike I would imagine spectators of the Kennedy assignation or 9-11. People remember vividly what they were doing on November 8, 2018. They recount how they evacuated and how long it took them to get out of town. Others recall the horrific flames chasing them as they drove out of town. I, too, share these memories; but I use them not to dwell on the tragic consequences of the fire, but as a tool to structure my new life.

The documentary about the Paradise Fire is now on Netflix. I honestly do not know if I can watch it. I watched part of the trailers and it was just too painful. The images of the flames and the sounds of people screaming still haunt me every night when I close my eyes. I know this too shall pass and I am utilizing meditation techniques during the day to quiet my mind.

Every morning as I write in my journal, I write one thing that I am grateful for. In the beginning, this was extremely difficult because what in the world could make me feel grateful? For crying out loud, I lost everything; I couldn't be with my mother for Christmas. Of course, I would remind myself that I was safe; my partner, Frank, and my cat were safe. We were blessed with the generosity of Frank's family. But I could not internalize the feelings of gratitude. My mother kept reminding me of what I once shared with her regarding pain after she broke her hip: "You should be grateful to be feeling your pain – I imagine Christopher Reeve, after his accident, would have relished the idea of feeling pain." In fact, when Mother was in the Emergency Room, the doctor asked if the pain was extensive, and she replied " Yes, Thank God I can feel it!"

Yes, it took some time for me to realize just how lucky I was to be alive. Lucky to have my fiancé's car in running condition. Lucky to have my precious cat safe (I can't even imagine all those animals that were left behind in the fire). And, of course, lucky to have the total support from family.

Looking back, our living conditions after the fire caused much amusement among my friends and family. While we were in Chico the night of the fire, we had to make a decision as to where to spend the night. My partner, Frank's ex-wife, and son lived in Northern California and we were told we would be welcome to stay there. So late that night we entered our temporary home, with our plastic bag of belongings. That night turned into one month! My Frank's ex-wife wife turned out to be one of the dearest people I have ever met. She became my confidant and staunch supporter during the roughest time of my life. We are good friends to this day.

As I slowly began my recovery process, I kept thinking of all those people still in tents and cars. Entire families displaced with nowhere to go. My friends suggested I use "Go Fund Me" to generate extra monies for us. There was no way I could that as we had good insurance; I began telling my friends if they wanted to help me, send money to the churches In Chico who were assisting the victims.

So now, the dust has settled, so to speak. I have a place to live, and I am financially stable. I published my first book. Now what? I have spent nearly on year in survivor mode, taking care of my physical, emotional, and mental needs. So much of my time was spent in nurturing my fiancé and myself. But, where do I go from here? I relived the fire in my book and now I can put it aside. I will not be stuck in the memory of the experience of the fire.

As I meditate, I think of what my future holds for me. I re-read the books from my favorite authors such as Deepak Chopra, Wayne Dyer, and the books on Abraham. I resonate to the wisdom passed down from Lao tzu; the wisdom which inspired my authors. Sometimes I am in such a quandary regarding my conflicting beliefs. All my life I had the erroneous belief that we need to be in control of our lives: Take charge! Make goals! Set objectives! And now I realize I am not in control of anything, even my emotions. So now my mantra becomes: let go. Let God.

But my mind still is in a turmoil with the Law of Attraction; did I attract disaster? What was my mindset before the fire? I do admit that the focus of my being was greed, constantly accumulating more "stuff" or "crap" as Frank would call it! My wardrobe and accessories filled three rooms; my antiques and books filled the remaining rooms. I realize now how my possessions defined who I was. My degrees and awards plastered the walls of my office to further define me. At the same time, I would voraciously read my spiritual books on living a simple life, letting go of material things, practicing detachment toward belongings. My friend who lost everything in the fire and I would discuss the concept of letting go; in fact, that was the premise of the book by Esther Hicks which we were perusing in our book club the week before the fire. How ironic that we did let go of everything but of course, it was not by choice.

Just this week, she confided to me that she sat down one afternoon and visualized the fire blazing through her home, all of her treasures going up in flames, one by one. Last night I watched "Eat Pray Love" and kept replaying the scene where the main characters were in Italy, discussing the grandeur of once what was Rome. They were in the ruins of a tomb and remarked "Ruin is a gift. Ruin is the road to transformation." (Elizabeth Gilbert) She also said "... maybe my life hasn't been so chaotic, it's just the world that is, and the real trap is getting attached to any of it."

The tragedy that I experienced has, in so many ways given me the courage to do things I never dreamed I was capable of. For most of my life I was insecure, hiding behind a mask that portrayed confidence and self-assurance. Each morning I would create a new mask to greet the world – my make-up and wardrobe so meticulously put together hid my inner self. Now I realize this is how most of us interact with each other: masks greeting masks. Billy Joel, in the Piano Man, summed this up "They're sharing a drink called loneliness but it's better than dinking alone." It's frightening to be vulnerable, to let others in. Since the fire, I don't have the mask I relied on; I am free of the pretense of hiding the real me. And it is truly amazing! I have courage which I suppose was hidden in the recesses of my insecurity and I somehow feel I have nothing to lose. (I have read that it is common for some survivors feel this way).

Maybe the catastrophe of the fire was not the major tragedy in my life. Maybe the tragedy of my life was my own demons- thoughts of insecurity and worry about how others viewed me, always trying to please others – kept me from embracing all that life had to offer me. Being older and wiser, I realize that when we are young, we worry about what people are thinking about us; when we are in our sixties, we realize they weren't thinking about us at all. My successes were hollow; I was never satisfied with what I had achieved. So many hours of the day were spent on ruminating about my mistakes, my perceived failures.

I realize I am far being unique in my self-perception. There are so many people out there, dealing with their inner demons. Hence, the rampant practice of self-medicating drugs and anti-depressants to help us get through the days and the long nights. For so many years, I thought I was the only one, berating herself for not completing goals, for making so mistakes. As I open up to those around me without my mask, I discover that everyone has their demons!

So, is it true that everything happens for a reason? Do we need a tragedy to transform our lives? Are the "ruins truly the road to transformation?" In my case, I have learned more about myself, especially the inner strength I never knew I had. I am in physical therapy with a therapist who truly believes in the mind-body connection. I am learning about how much of my body has stored all the stress (both self-imposed and fire-related) and is suffering leading to lack of sleep and muscle spasms. Our bodies are amazing! All of our aches and pains let the mind know that our past hurts and transgressions need to be dealt with. We have become so adept at repressing our pain, or ignoring it all together by taking pills. Our bodies never "forget" the stresses forced upon it. I am now just understanding how my poor body has been trying to tell me to adopt a different lifestyle: one of self-acceptance and nurturing.

Frank is a perfect example of repressing pain. His initial reaction was numbness which quickly turned into anger. He could not verbalize his pain, his sense of loss. Paradise had been his dream: he had relished the idea sitting on his back deck watching the deer roam in our yard, and being one with nature. In every conversation, he would make reference to some object that got destroyed in the fire: "I have 2 ladders. They are in the garage," "I have a new set of golf clubs, they are..." His body reacted to this anger: He eventually could not turn his head; he had limited motion in his arms. He had difficulty sleeping because of the pain in his neck. He is still in physical therapy, trying to regain movement. His coping mechanism is to not discuss his feelings, on rare occasions he will admit to his depression.

Repressing pain can really take its toll on those recovering from a catastrophe. When we moved to Paradise in July of 2018, we were fortunate to have a wonderful couple as our next door neighbors. They were involved in the community and church, always ready to help others. When I got the phone call that my mother had fallen, they drove me to Sacramento in order that I could be with her that evening. They were planning on travelling throughout the states in their new RV once their house sold. They sold their home, put their furniture in storage, and the rest of their belongings in their RV. The new family was to move in the second week of November. On the day of the fire, their RV was engulfed in flames; but they were able to make their escape out of town. In the past the year both of them suffered not only emotionally, but also physically. My neighbor's wife had good health before the fire; now she has been diagnosed with uncontrollable acute hypertension and anxiety disorder. She spent 3 days in ICU and now has AFib (Atrial Fibrillation). Her husband had to have a new pacemaker put in due to the stress and anxiety. The two of them coped by first, immersing themselves in a house that needed a complete overhaul. When it was completed, they worked on the five acres of land from sun up to sundown. When that was done, they travelled in their RV for three months. They admitted that they are still "running" running from anything that will remind them of the fire, running from friends because she doesn't want to reveal her pain. They have isolated themselves on the property where they don't have to get involved with anybody. The wife "sees" fire in many daily occurrences – a red sunset, smoke in the air – and she relives the actual fire all over again. Her nightmares mirror mine – being stuck on the road out of Paradise, flames chasing us, but we are not moving. The classic anxiety nightmare. I think her experiences in the aftermath of the fire are so tragic as she lost that infectious vitality that defined her. I can only pray that she can recover

I was able to interview another survivor who will not buy any furniture or belongings outside of her clothing and basic needs. She rents a room and insists that she is afraid of becoming attached to anything or anybody because if they were gone, she wouldn't "make it."

Each one of us has a personal story to tell, how we go through the stages of recovery. I would hope that many of us can move forward. Maybe that is easy for me to say as I did not lose a relative, pet or friend. Would I be able to move forward if I did lose someone dear to me? Of course, I will never know the answer to that, except I pray that if that were to happen, I would have the support system of my faith, family, and friends. Writing has become my best therapy: I am able to sort out my confusing and painful thoughts, keep still to listen to my body and reflect on my actions – of course, my therapist insists that I spend more time doing absolutely nothing and not overly think about everything. I think I can manage that.

So, the journey I have embarked on since the fire is really quite exciting! With my newly gained insights,

I can physically, as well as mentally and emotionally, heal. I take risks I would have never attempted before: reaching out to other people for help, teaching in classes where students have severe behavioral problems, and yes, writing and publishing books. I have no idea where my journey is headed, and that is okay. "let go; Let God"

ABOUT THE BOOK

"Smoldering Ashes Of Paradise" is the sequel to "Phoenix Rising From the Ashes." It takes the reader on the continued journey of transformation. It is a poignant story of how the author and other victims cope with catastrophe. All of us, at one time or another face daunting challenges in our lives, and it is how we meet them that determines our ability to be transformed by them. The Paradise Fire is remembered as a catastrophe that destroyed an entire town, but as survivors, we must not remember the fire as destroying us.

Printed in the United States
By Bookmasters